THE CATEGORIES

ARISTOTLE

Published by True Sign Publishing House
Address: SY. No. 21/2 & 21/3, Sonnenahalli,
Krishnarajapura, Bengaluru,
Karnataka - 560049 India
E-mail: truesignbooks@gmail.com
Website: www.truesign.in

The Categories
Author: Aristotle

ISBN: 978-93-5584-080-6

First Edition: 2022

Contents

SECTION-1

Part-1

Things are said to be named 'equivocally' when, though they have a common name, the definition corresponding with the name differs for each. Thus, a real man and a figure in a picture can both lay claim to the name 'animal'; yet these are equivocally so named, for, though they have a common name, the definition corresponding with the name differs for each. For should any one define in what sense each is an animal, his definition in the one case will be appropriate to that case only.

On the other hand, things are said to be named 'univocally' which have both the name and the definition answering to the name in common. A man and an ox are both 'animal', and these are univocally so named, inasmuch as not only the name, but also the definition, is the same in both cases: for if a man should state in what sense each is an animal, the statement in the one case would be identical with that in the other.

Things are said to be named 'derivatively', which derive their name from some other name, but differ from it in termination. Thus the grammarian derives his name from the word 'grammar', and the courageous man from the word 'courage'.

Part-2

Forms of speech are either simple or composite. Examples of the latter are such expressions as 'the man runs', 'the man wins'; of the former 'man', 'ox', 'runs', 'wins'.

Of things themselves some are predicable of a subject, and are never present in a subject. Thus 'man' is predicable of the individual man, and is never present in a subject.

By being 'present in a subject' I do not mean present as parts are present in a whole, but being incapable of existence apart from the said subject.

Some things, again, are present in a subject, but are never predicable of a subject. For instance, a certain point of grammatical knowledge is present in the mind, but is not predicable of any subject; or again, a certain whiteness may be present in the body (for colour requires a material basis), yet it is never predicable of anything.

Other things, again, are both predicable of a subject and present in a subject. Thus while knowledge is present in the human mind, it is predicable of grammar.

There is, lastly, a class of things which are neither present in a subject nor predicable of a subject, such as the individual man or the individual horse. But, to speak more generally, that which is individual and has the character of a unit is never predicable of a subject. Yet in some cases there is nothing to prevent such being present in a subject. Thus a certain point of grammatical knowledge is present in a subject.

Part-3

When one thing is predicated of another, all that which is predicable of the predicate will be predicable also of the subject. Thus, 'man' is predicated of the individual man; but 'animal' is predicated of 'man'; it will, therefore, be predicable of the individual man also: for the individual man is both 'man' and 'animal'.

If genera are different and co-ordinate, their differentiae are themselves different in kind. Take as an instance the genus 'animal' and the genus 'knowledge'. 'With feet', 'two-footed', 'winged', 'aquatic', are differentiae of 'animal'; the species of knowledge are not distinguished by the same differentiae. One species of knowledge does not differ from another in being 'two-footed'.

But where one genus is subordinate to another, there is nothing to prevent their having the same differentiae: for the greater class is predicated of the lesser, so that all the differentiae of the predicate will be differentiae also of the subject.

Part-4

Expressions which are in no way composite signify substance, quantity, quality, relation, place, time, position, state, action, or affection. To sketch my meaning roughly, examples of substance are 'man' or 'the horse', of quantity, such terms as 'two cubits long' or 'three cubits long', of quality, such attributes as 'white', 'grammatical'. 'Double', 'half', 'greater', fall under the category of relation; 'in the market place', 'in the Lyceum', under that of place; 'yesterday', 'last year', under that of time. 'Lying', 'sitting', are terms indicating position, 'shod', 'armed', state; 'to lance', 'to cauterize', action; 'to be lanced', 'to be cauterized', affection.

No one of these terms, in and by itself, involves an affirmation; it is by the combination of such terms that positive or negative statements arise. For every assertion must, as is admitted, be either true or false, whereas expressions which are not in any way composite such as 'man', 'white', 'runs', 'wins', cannot be either true or false.

Part-5

Substance, in the truest and primary and most definite sense of the word, is that which is neither predicable of a subject nor present in a subject; for instance, the individual man or horse. But in a secondary sense those things are called substances within which, as species, the primary substances are included; also those which, as genera, include the species. For instance, the individual man is included in the species 'man', and the genus to which the species belongs is 'animal'; these, therefore—that is to say, the species 'man' and the genus 'animal,-are termed secondary substances.

It is plain from what has been said that both the name and the definition of the predicate must be predicable of the subject. For instance, 'man' is predicated of the individual man. Now in this case the name of the species 'man' is applied to the individual, for we use the term 'man' in describing the individual; and the definition of 'man' will also be predicated of the individual man, for the individual man is both man and animal. Thus, both the name and the definition of the species are predicable of the individual.

With regard, on the other hand, to those things which are present in a subject, it is generally the case that neither their name nor their definition is predicable of that in which they are present. Though, however, the definition is never predicable, there is nothing in certain cases to prevent the name being used. For instance, 'white' being present in a body is predicated of that in which it is present, for a body is called white: the definition, however, of the colour 'white' is never predicable of the body.

Everything except primary substances is either predicable of a primary substance or present in a primary substance. This becomes evident by reference to particular instances which occur. 'Animal' is predicated of the species 'man', therefore of the individual man, for if there were no individual man of whom it could be predicated, it could not be predicated of the species 'man' at all. Again, colour is present in body, therefore in individual bodies, for if there were no individual body in which it was present, it could not be present in body at all. Thus everything except primary substances is either predicated of primary substances, or is present in them, and if these last did not exist, it would be impossible for anything else to exist.

Of secondary substances, the species is more truly substance than the genus, being more nearly related to primary substance. For if any one should render an account of what a primary substance is, he would render a more instructive account, and one more proper to the subject, by stating the species than by stating the genus. Thus, he would give a more instructive account of an individual man by stating that he was man than by stating that he was animal, for the former description is peculiar to the individual in a greater degree, while the latter is too general. Again, the man who gives an account of the nature of an individual tree will give a more instructive account by mentioning the species 'tree' than by mentioning the genus 'plant'.

Moreover, primary substances are most properly called substances in virtue of the fact that they are the entities which underlie everything else, and that everything else is either predicated of them or present in them. Now the same relation which subsists between primary substance and everything else subsists also between the species and the genus: for the species is to the genus as subject is to predicate, since the genus is predicated of the species, whereas the species cannot be predicated of the genus. Thus we have a second ground for asserting that the species is more truly substance than the genus.

Of species themselves, except in the case of such as are genera, no one is more truly substance than another. We should not give a more appropriate account of the individual man by stating the species to which he belonged, than we should of an individual horse by adopting the same method of definition. In the same way, of primary substances, no one is more truly substance than another; an individual man is not more truly substance than an individual ox.

It is, then, with good reason that of all that remains, when we exclude primary substances, we concede to species and genera alone the name 'secondary substance', for these alone of all the predicates convey a knowledge of primary substance. For it is by stating the species or the genus that we appropriately define any individual man; and we shall make our definition more exact by stating the former than by stating the latter. All other things that we state, such as that he is white, that he runs, and so on, are irrelevant to the definition. Thus it is just that these alone, apart from primary substances, should be called substances.

Further, primary substances are most properly so called, because they underlie and are the subjects of everything else. Now the same relation that subsists between primary substance and everything else subsists also between the species and the genus to which the primary substance belongs, on the one hand, and every attribute which is not included within these, on the other. For these are the subjects of all such. If we call an individual man 'skilled in grammar', the predicate is applicable also to the species and to the genus to which he belongs. This law holds good in all cases.

It is a common characteristic of all substance that it is never present in a subject. For primary substance is neither present in a subject nor predicated of a subject; while, with regard to secondary substances, it is clear from the following arguments (apart from others) that they are not present in a subject. For 'man' is predicated of the individual man, but is not present in any subject: for manhood is not present in the individual man. In the same way, 'animal' is also predicated of the individual man, but is not present in him. Again, when a thing is present in a subject, though the name may quite well be applied to that in which it is present, the definition cannot be applied. Yet of secondary substances, not only the name, but also the definition, applies to the subject: we should use both the definition of the species and that of the genus with reference to the individual man. Thus substance cannot be present in a subject.

Yet this is not peculiar to substance, for it is also the case that differentiae cannot be present in subjects. The characteristics 'terrestrial' and 'two-footed' are predicated of the species 'man', but not present in it. For they are not in man. Moreover, the definition of the differentia may be predicated of that of which the differentia itself is predicated. For instance, if the characteristic 'terrestrial' is predicated of the species 'man', the definition also of that characteristic may be used to form the predicate of the species 'man': for 'man' is terrestrial.

The fact that the parts of substances appear to be present in the whole, as in a subject, should not make us apprehensive lest we should have to admit that such parts are not substances: for in explaining the phrase 'being present in a subject', we stated' that we meant 'otherwise than as parts in a whole'.

It is the mark of substances and of differentiae that, in all propositions of which they form the predicate, they are predicated univocally. For all such propositions have for their subject either the individual or the species. It is true that, inasmuch as primary substance is not predicable of anything, it can never form the predicate of any proposition. But of secondary substances, the species is predicated of the individual, the genus both of the species and of the individual. Similarly the differentiae are predicated of the species and of the individuals. Moreover, the definition of the species and that of the genus are applicable to the primary substance, and that of the genus to the species. For all that is predicated of the predicate will be predicated also of the subject. Similarly, the definition of the differentiae will be applicable to the species and to the individuals. But it was stated above that the word 'univocal' was applied to those things which had both name and definition in common. It is, therefore, established that in every proposition, of which either substance or a differentia forms the predicate, these are predicated univocally.

All substance appears to signify that which is individual. In the case of primary substance this is indisputably true, for the thing is a unit. In the case of secondary substances, when we speak, for instance, of 'man' or 'animal', our form of speech gives the impression that we are here also indicating that which is individual, but the impression is not strictly true; for a secondary substance is not an individual, but a class with a certain qualification; for it is not one and single as a primary substance is; the words 'man', 'animal', are predicable of more than one subject.

Yet species and genus do not merely indicate quality, like the term 'white'; 'white' indicates quality and nothing further, but species and genus determine the quality with reference to a substance: they signify substance qualitatively differentiated. The determinate qualification covers a larger field in the case of the genus that in that of the species: he who uses the word 'animal' is herein using a word of wider extension than he who uses the word 'man'.

Another mark of substance is that it has no contrary. What could be the contrary of any primary substance, such as the individual man or animal? It has none. Nor can the species or the genus have a contrary. Yet this characteristic is not peculiar to substance, but is true of many other things, such as quantity. There is nothing that forms the contrary of 'two cubits long' or of 'three cubits long', or of 'ten', or of any such term. A man may contend that 'much' is the contrary of 'little', or 'great' of 'small', but of definite quantitative terms no contrary exists.

Substance, again, does not appear to admit of variation of degree. I do not mean by this that one substance cannot be more or less truly substance than another, for it has already been stated that this is the case; but that no single substance admits of varying degrees within itself. For instance, one particular substance, 'man', cannot be more or less man either than himself at some other time or than some other man. One man cannot be more man than another, as that which is white may be more or less white than some other white object, or as that which is beautiful may be more or less beautiful than some other beautiful object. The same quality, moreover, is said to subsist in a thing in varying degrees at different times. A body, being white, is said to be whiter at one time than it was before, or, being warm, is said to be warmer or less warm than at some other time. But substance is not said to be more or less that which it is: a man is not more truly a man at one time than he was before, nor is anything, if it is substance, more or less what it is. Substance, then, does not admit of variation of degree.

The most distinctive mark of substance appears to be that, while remaining numerically one and the same, it is capable of admitting contrary qualities. From among things other than substance, we should find ourselves unable to bring forward any which possessed this mark. Thus, one and the same colour cannot be white and black. Nor can the same one action be good and bad: this law holds good with everything that is not substance. But one and the selfsame substance, while retaining its identity, is yet capable of admitting contrary qualities. The same individual person is at one time white, at another black, at one time warm, at another cold, at one time good, at another bad. This capacity is found nowhere else, though it might be maintained that a statement or opinion was an exception to the rule. The same statement, it is agreed, can be both true and false. For if the statement 'he is sitting' is true, yet, when the person in question has risen, the same statement will be false. The same applies to opinions. For if any one thinks truly that a person is sitting, yet, when that person has risen, this same opinion, if still held, will be false. Yet although this exception may be allowed, there is, nevertheless, a difference in the manner in which the thing takes place. It is by themselves changing that substances admit contrary qualities. It is thus that that which was hot becomes cold, for it has entered into a different state. Similarly that which was white becomes black, and that which was bad good, by a process of change; and in the same way in all other cases it is by changing that substances are capable of admitting contrary qualities. But statements and opinions themselves remain unaltered in all respects: it is by the alteration in the facts of the case that the contrary quality comes to be theirs. The statement 'he is sitting' remains unaltered, but it is at one time true, at another false, according to circumstances. What has been said of statements applies also to opinions. Thus, in respect of the manner in which the thing takes place, it is the peculiar mark of substance that it should be capable of admitting contrary qualities; for it is by itself changing that it does so.

If, then, a man should make this exception and contend that statements and opinions are capable of admitting contrary qualities, his contention is unsound. For statements and opinions are said to have this capacity, not because they themselves undergo modification, but because this modification occurs in the case of something else. The truth or falsity of a statement depends on facts, and not on any power on the part of the statement itself of admitting contrary qualities. In short, there is nothing which can alter the nature of statements and opinions. As, then, no change takes place in themselves, these cannot be said to be capable of admitting contrary qualities.

But it is by reason of the modification which takes place within the substance itself that a substance is said to be capable of admitting contrary qualities; for a substance admits within itself either disease or health, whiteness or blackness. It is in this sense that it is said to be capable of admitting contrary qualities.

To sum up, it is a distinctive mark of substance, that, while remaining numerically one and the same, it is capable of admitting contrary qualities, the modification taking place through a change in the substance itself.

Let these remarks suffice on the subject of substance.

Part-6

Quantity is either discrete or continuous. Moreover, some quantities are such that each part of the whole has a relative position to the other parts: others have within them no such relation of part to part.

Instances of discrete quantities are number and speech; of continuous, lines, surfaces, solids, and, besides these, time and place.

In the case of the parts of a number, there is no common boundary at which they join. For example: two fives make ten, but the two fives have no common boundary, but are separate; the parts three and seven also do not join at any boundary. Nor, to generalize, would it ever be possible in the case of number that there should be a common boundary among the parts; they are always separate. Number, therefore, is a discrete quantity.

The same is true of speech. That speech is a quantity is evident: for it is measured in long and short syllables. I mean here that speech which is vocal. Moreover, it is a discrete quantity for its parts have no common boundary. There is no common boundary at which the syllables join, but each is separate and distinct from the rest.

A line, on the other hand, is a continuous quantity, for it is possible to find a common boundary at which its parts join. In the case of the line, this common boundary is the point; in the case of the plane, it is the line: for the parts of the plane have also a common boundary. Similarly you can find a common boundary in the case of the parts of a solid, namely either a line or a plane.

Space and time also belong to this class of quantities. Time, past, present, and future, forms a continuous whole. Space, likewise, is a continuous quantity; for the parts of a solid occupy a certain space, and these have a common boundary; it follows that the parts of space also, which are occupied by the parts of the solid, have the same common boundary as the parts of the solid. Thus, not only time, but space also, is a continuous quantity, for its parts have a common boundary.

Quantities consist either of parts which bear a relative position each to each, or of parts which do not. The parts of a line bear a relative position to each other, for each lies somewhere, and it would be possible to distinguish each, and to state the position of each on the plane and to explain to what sort of part among the rest each was contiguous. Similarly the parts of a plane have position, for it could similarly be stated what was the position of each and what sort of parts were contiguous. The same is true with regard to the solid and to space. But it would be impossible to show that the parts of a number had a relative position each to each, or a particular position, or to state what parts were contiguous. Nor could this be done in the case of time, for none of the parts of time has an abiding existence, and that which does not abide can hardly have position. It would be better to say that such parts had a relative order, in virtue of one being prior to another. Similarly with number: in counting, 'one' is prior to 'two', and 'two' to 'three', and thus the parts of number may be said to possess a relative order, though it would be impossible to discover any distinct position for each. This holds good also in the case of speech. None of its parts has an abiding existence: when once a syllable is pronounced, it is not possible to retain it, so that, naturally, as the parts do not abide, they cannot have position. Thus, some quantities consist of parts which have position, and some of those which have not.

Strictly speaking, only the things which I have mentioned belong to the category of quantity: everything else that is called quantitative is a quantity in a secondary sense. It is because we have in mind some one of these quantities, properly so called, that we apply quantitative terms to other things. We speak of what is white as large, because the surface over which the white extends is large; we speak of an action or a process as lengthy, because the time covered is long; these things cannot in their own right claim the quantitative epithet. For instance, should any one explain how long an action was, his statement would be made in terms of the time taken, to the effect that it lasted a year, or something of that sort. In the same way, he would explain the size of a white object in terms of surface, for he would state the area which it covered. Thus the things already mentioned, and these alone, are in their intrinsic nature quantities; nothing else can claim the name in its own right, but, if at all, only in a secondary sense.

Quantities have no contraries. In the case of definite quantities this is obvious; thus, there is nothing that is the contrary of 'two cubits long' or of 'three cubits long', or of a surface, or of any such quantities. A man might, indeed, argue that 'much' was the contrary of 'little', and 'great' of 'small'. But these are not quantitative, but relative; things are not great or small absolutely, they are so called rather as the result of an act of comparison. For instance, a mountain is called small, a grain large, in virtue of the fact that the latter is greater than others of its kind, the former less. Thus there is a reference here to an external standard, for if the terms 'great' and 'small' were used absolutely, a mountain would never be called small or a grain large. Again, we say that there are many people in a village, and few in Athens, although those in the city are many times as numerous as those in the village: or we say that a house has many in it, and a theatre few, though those in the theatre far outnumber those in the house. The terms 'two cubits long', 'three cubits long', and so on indicate quantity, the terms 'great' and 'small' indicate relation, for they have reference to an external standard. It is, therefore, plain that these are to be classed as relative.

Again, whether we define them as quantitative or not, they have no contraries: for how can there be a contrary of an attribute which is not to be apprehended in or by itself, but only by reference to something external? Again, if 'great' and 'small' are contraries, it will come about that the same subject can admit contrary qualities at one and the same time, and that things will themselves be contrary to themselves. For it happens at times that the same thing is both small and great. For the same thing may be small in comparison with one thing, and great in comparison with another, so that the same thing comes to be both small and great at one and the same time, and is of such a nature as to admit contrary qualities at one and the same moment. Yet it was agreed, when substance was being discussed, that nothing admits contrary qualities at one and the same moment. For though substance is capable of admitting contrary qualities, yet no one is at the same time both sick and healthy, nothing is at the same time both white and black. Nor is there anything which is qualified in contrary ways at one and the same time.

Moreover, if these were contraries, they would themselves be contrary to themselves. For if 'great' is the contrary of 'small', and the same thing is both great and small at the same time, then 'small' or 'great' is the contrary of itself. But this is impossible. The term 'great', therefore, is not the contrary of the term 'small', nor 'much' of 'little'. And even though a man should call these terms not relative but quantitative, they would not have contraries.

It is in the case of space that quantity most plausibly appears to admit of a contrary. For men define the term 'above' as the contrary of 'below', when it is the region at the centre they mean by 'below'; and this is so, because nothing is farther from the extremities of the universe than the region at the centre. Indeed, it seems that in defining contraries of every kind men have recourse to a spatial metaphor, for they say that those things are contraries which, within the same class, are separated by the greatest possible distance.

Quantity does not, it appears, admit of variation of degree. One thing cannot be two cubits long in a greater degree than another. Similarly with regard to number: what is 'three' is not more truly three than what is 'five' is five; nor is one set of three more truly three than another set. Again, one period of time is not said to be more truly time than another. Nor is there any other kind of quantity, of all that have been mentioned, with regard to which variation of degree can be predicated. The category of quantity, therefore, does not admit of variation of degree.

The most distinctive mark of quantity is that equality and inequality are predicated of it. Each of the aforesaid quantities is said to be equal or unequal. For instance, one solid is said to be equal or unequal to another; number, too, and time can have these terms applied to them, indeed can all those kinds of quantity that have been mentioned.

That which is not a quantity can by no means, it would seem, be termed equal or unequal to anything else. One particular disposition or one particular quality, such as whiteness, is by no means compared with another in terms of equality and inequality but rather in terms of similarity. Thus it is the distinctive mark of quantity that it can be called equal and unequal.

SECTION-2

Part-7

Those things are called relative, which, being either said to be of something else or related to something else, are explained by reference to that other thing. For instance, the word 'superior' is explained by reference to something else, for it is superiority over something else that is meant. Similarly, the expression 'double' has this external reference, for it is the double of something else that is meant. So it is with everything else of this kind. There are, moreover, other relatives, e.g. habit, disposition, perception, knowledge, and attitude. The significance of all these is explained by a reference to something else and in no other way. Thus, a habit is a habit of something, knowledge is knowledge of something, attitude is the attitude of something. So it is with all other relatives that have been mentioned. Those terms, then, are called relative, the nature of which is explained by reference to something else, the preposition 'of' or some other preposition being used to indicate the relation. Thus, one mountain is called great in comparison with another; for the mountain claims this attribute by comparison with something. Again, that which is called similar must be similar to something else, and all other such attributes have this external reference. It is to be noted that lying and standing and sitting are particular attitudes, but attitude is itself a relative term. To lie, to stand, to be seated, are not themselves attitudes, but take their name from the aforesaid attitudes.

It is possible for relatives to have contraries. Thus virtue has a contrary, vice, these both being relatives; knowledge, too, has a contrary, ignorance. But this is not the mark of all relatives; 'double' and 'triple' have no contrary, nor indeed has any such term.

It also appears that relatives can admit of variation of degree. For 'like' and 'unlike', 'equal' and 'unequal', have the modifications 'more' and 'less' applied to them, and each of these is relative in character: for the terms 'like' and 'unequal' bear a reference to something external. Yet, again, it is not every relative term that admits of variation of degree. No term such as 'double' admits of this modification. All relatives have correlatives: by the term 'slave' we mean the slave of a master, by the term 'master', the master of a slave; by 'double', the double of its half; by 'half', the half of its double; by 'greater', greater than that which is less; by 'less', less than that which is greater.

So it is with every other relative term; but the case we use to express the correlation differs in some instances. Thus, by knowledge we mean knowledge of the knowable; by the knowable, that which is to be apprehended by knowledge; by perception, perception of the perceptible; by the perceptible, that which is apprehended by perception.

Sometimes, however, reciprocity of correlation does not appear to exist. This comes about when a blunder is made, and that to which the relative is related is not accurately stated. If a man states that a wing is necessarily relative to a bird, the connexion between these two will not be reciprocal, for it will not be possible to say that a bird is a bird by reason of its wings. The reason is that the original statement was inaccurate, for the wing is not said to be relative to the bird qua bird, since many creatures besides birds have wings, but qua winged creature. If, then, the statement is made accurate, the connexion will be reciprocal, for we can speak of a wing, having reference necessarily to a winged creature, and of a winged creature as being such because of its wings.

Occasionally, perhaps, it is necessary to coin words, if no word exists by which a correlation can adequately be explained. If we define a rudder as necessarily having reference to a boat, our definition will not be appropriate, for the rudder does not have this reference to a boat qua boat, as there are boats which have no rudders. Thus we cannot use the terms reciprocally, for the word 'boat' cannot be said to find its explanation in the word 'rudder'. As there is no existing word, our definition would perhaps be more accurate if we coined some word like 'ruddered' as the correlative of 'rudder'. If we express ourselves thus accurately, at any rate the terms are reciprocally connected, for the 'ruddered' thing is 'ruddered' in virtue of its rudder. So it is in all other cases. A head will be more accurately defined as the correlative of that which is 'headed', than as that of an animal, for the animal does not have a head qua animal, since many animals have no head.

Thus we may perhaps most easily comprehend that to which a thing is related, when a name does not exist, if, from that which has a name, we derive a new name, and apply it to that with which the first is reciprocally connected, as in the aforesaid instances, when we derived the word 'winged' from 'wing' and from 'rudder'.

All relatives, then, if properly defined, have a correlative. I add this condition because, if that to which they are related is stated as haphazard and not accurately, the two are not found to be interdependent. Let me state what I mean more clearly. Even in the case of acknowledged correlatives, and where names exist for each, there will be no interdependence if one of the two is denoted, not by that name which expresses the correlative notion, but by one of irrelevant significance. The term 'slave', if defined as related, not to a master, but to a man, or a biped, or anything of that sort, is not reciprocally connected with that in relation to which it is defined, for the statement is not exact. Further, if one thing is said to be correlative with another, and the terminology used is correct, then, though all irrelevant attributes should be removed, and only that one attribute left in virtue of which it was correctly stated to be correlative with that other, the stated correlation will still exist. If the correlative of 'the slave' is said to be 'the master', then, though all irrelevant attributes of the said 'master', such as 'biped', 'receptive of knowledge', 'human', should be removed, and the attribute 'master' alone left, the stated correlation existing between him and the slave will remain the same, for it is of a master that a slave is said to be the slave. On the other hand, if, of two correlatives, one is not correctly termed, then, when all other attributes are removed and that alone is left in virtue of which it was stated to be correlative, the stated correlation will be found to have disappeared.

For suppose the correlative of 'the slave' should be said to be 'the man', or the correlative of 'the wing' is 'the bird'; if the attribute 'master' be withdrawn from 'the man', the correlation between 'the man' and 'the slave' will cease to exist, for if the man is not a master, the slave is not a slave. Similarly, if the attribute 'winged' be withdrawn from 'the bird', 'the wing' will no longer be relative; for if the so-called correlative is not winged, it follows that 'the wing' has no correlative.

Thus it is essential that the correlated terms should be exactly designated; if there is a name existing, the statement will be easy; if not, it is doubtless our duty to construct names. When the terminology is thus correct, it is evident that all correlatives are interdependent.

Correlatives are thought to come into existence simultaneously. This is for the most part true, as in the case of the double and the half. The existence of the half necessitates the existence of that of which it is a half. Similarly the existence of a master necessitates the existence of a slave, and that of a slave implies that of a master; these are merely instances of a general rule. Moreover, they cancel one another; for if there is no double it follows that there is no half, and vice versa; this rule also applies to all such correlatives. Yet it does not appear to be true in all cases that correlatives come into existence simultaneously. The object of knowledge would appear to exist before knowledge itself, for it is usually the case that we acquire knowledge of objects already existing; it would be difficult, if not impossible, to find a branch of knowledge the beginning of the existence of which was contemporaneous with that of its object.

Again, while the object of knowledge, if it ceases to exist, cancels at the same time the knowledge which was its correlative, the converse of this is not true. It is true that if the object of knowledge does not exist there can be no knowledge: for there will no longer be anything to know. Yet it is equally true that, if knowledge of a certain object does not exist, the object may nevertheless quite well exist. Thus, in the case of the squaring of the circle, if indeed that process is an object of knowledge, though it itself exists as an object of knowledge, yet the knowledge of it has not yet come into existence. Again, if all animals ceased to exist, there would be no knowledge, but there might yet be many objects of knowledge.

This is likewise the case with regard to perception: for the object of perception is, it appears, prior to the act of perception. If the perceptible is annihilated, perception also will cease to exist; but the annihilation of perception does not cancel the existence of the perceptible. For perception implies a body perceived and a body in which perception takes place. Now if that which is perceptible is annihilated, it follows that the body is annihilated, for the body is a perceptible thing; and if the body does not exist, it follows that perception also ceases to exist. Thus the annihilation of the perceptible involves that of perception.

But the annihilation of perception does not involve that of the perceptible. For if the animal is annihilated, it follows that perception also is annihilated, but perceptibles such as body, heat, sweetness, bitterness, and so on, will remain.

Again, perception is generated at the same time as the perceiving subject, for it comes into existence at the same time as the animal. But the perceptible surely exists before perception; for fire and water and such elements, out of which the animal is itself composed, exist before the animal is an animal at all, and before perception. Thus it would seem that the perceptible exists before perception.

It may be questioned whether it is true that no substance is relative, as seems to be the case, or whether exception is to be made in the case of certain secondary substances. With regard to primary substances, it is quite true that there is no such possibility, for neither wholes nor parts of primary substances are relative. The individual man or ox is not defined with reference to something external. Similarly with the parts: a particular hand or head is not defined as a particular hand or head of a particular person, but as the hand or head of a particular person. It is true also, for the most part at least, in the case of secondary substances; the species 'man' and the species 'ox' are not defined with reference to anything outside themselves. Wood, again, is only relative in so far as it is some one's property, not in so far as it is wood. It is plain, then, that in the cases mentioned substance is not relative. But with regard to some secondary substances there is a difference of opinion; thus, such terms as 'head' and 'hand' are defined with reference to that of which the things indicated are a part, and so it comes about that these appear to have a relative character. Indeed, if our definition of that which is relative was complete, it is very difficult, if not impossible, to prove that no substance is relative. If, however, our definition was not complete, if those things only are properly called relative in the case of which relation to an external object is a necessary condition of existence, perhaps some explanation of the dilemma may be found.

The former definition does indeed apply to all relatives, but the fact that a thing is explained with reference to something else does not make it essentially relative.

From this it is plain that, if a man definitely apprehends a relative thing, he will also definitely apprehend that to which it is relative. Indeed this is self-evident: for if a man knows that some particular thing is relative, assuming that we call that a relative in the case of which relation to something is a necessary condition of existence, he knows that also to which it is related. For if he does not know at all that to which it is related, he will not know whether or not it is relative. This is clear, moreover, in particular instances. If a man knows definitely that such and such a thing is 'double', he will also forthwith know definitely that of which it is the double. For if there is nothing definite of which he knows it to be the double, he does not know at all that it is double. Again, if he knows that a thing is more beautiful, it follows necessarily that he will forthwith definitely know that also than which it is more beautiful. He will not merely know indefinitely that it is more beautiful than something which is less beautiful, for this would be supposition, not knowledge. For if he does not know definitely that than which it is more beautiful, he can no longer claim to know definitely that it is more beautiful than something else which is less beautiful: for it might be that nothing was less beautiful. It is, therefore, evident that if a man apprehends some relative thing definitely, he necessarily knows that also definitely to which it is related.

Now the head, the hand, and such things are substances, and it is possible to know their essential character definitely, but it does not necessarily follow that we should know that to which they are related. It is not possible to know forthwith whose head or hand is meant. Thus these are not relatives, and, this being the case, it would be true to say that no substance is relative in character. It is perhaps a difficult matter, in such cases, to make a positive statement without more exhaustive examination, but to have raised questions with regard to details is not without advantage.

Part-8

By 'quality' I mean that in virtue of which people are said to be such and such.

Quality is a term that is used in many senses. One sort of quality let us call 'habit' or 'disposition'. Habit differs from disposition in being more lasting and more firmly established. The various kinds of knowledge and of virtue are habits, for knowledge, even when acquired only in a moderate degree, is, it is agreed, abiding in its character and difficult to displace, unless some great mental upheaval takes place, through disease or any such cause. The virtues, also, such as justice, self-restraint, and so on, are not easily dislodged or dismissed, so as to give place to vice.

By a disposition, on the other hand, we mean a condition that is easily changed and quickly gives place to its opposite. Thus, heat, cold, disease, health, and so on are dispositions. For a man is disposed in one way or another with reference to these, but quickly changes, becoming cold instead of warm, ill instead of well. So it is with all other dispositions also, unless through lapse of time a disposition has itself become inveterate and almost impossible to dislodge: in which case we should perhaps go so far as to call it a habit.

It is evident that men incline to call those conditions habits which are of a more or less permanent type and difficult to displace; for those who are not retentive of knowledge, but volatile, are not said to have such and such a 'habit' as regards knowledge, yet they are disposed, we may say, either better or worse, towards knowledge. Thus habit differs from disposition in this, that while the latter in ephemeral, the former is permanent and difficult to alter.

Habits are at the same time dispositions, but dispositions are not necessarily habits. For those who have some specific habit may be said also, in virtue of that habit, to be thus or thus disposed; but those who are disposed in some specific way have not in all cases the corresponding habit.

Another sort of quality is that in virtue of which, for example, we call men good boxers or runners, or healthy or sickly: in fact it includes all those terms which refer to inborn capacity or incapacity. Such things are not predicated of a person in virtue of his disposition, but in virtue of his inborn capacity or incapacity to do something with ease or to avoid defeat of any kind. Persons are called good boxers or good runners, not in virtue of such and such a disposition, but in virtue of an inborn capacity to accomplish something with ease. Men are called healthy in virtue of the inborn capacity of easy resistance to those unhealthy influences that may ordinarily arise; unhealthy, in virtue of the lack of this capacity. Similarly with regard to softness and hardness. Hardness is predicated of a thing because it has that capacity of resistance which enables it to withstand disintegration; softness, again, is predicated of a thing by reason of the lack of that capacity.

A third class within this category is that of affective qualities and affections. Sweetness, bitterness, sourness, are examples of this sort of quality, together with all that is akin to these; heat, moreover, and cold, whiteness, and blackness are affective qualities. It is evident that these are qualities, for those things that possess them are themselves said to be such and such by reason of their presence. Honey is called sweet because it contains sweetness; the body is called white because it contains whiteness; and so in all other cases.

The term 'affective quality' is not used as indicating that those things which admit these qualities are affected in any way. Honey is not called sweet because it is affected in a specific way, nor is this what is meant in any other instance. Similarly heat and cold are called affective qualities, not because those things which admit them are affected. What is meant is that these said qualities are capable of producing an 'affection' in the way of perception. For sweetness has the power of affecting the sense of taste; heat, that of touch; and so it is with the rest of these qualities.

Whiteness and blackness, however, and the other colours, are not said to be affective qualities in this sense, but because they themselves are the results of an affection. It is plain that many changes of colour take place because of affections. When a man is ashamed, he blushes; when he is afraid, he becomes pale, and so on. So true is this, that when a man is by nature liable to such affections, arising from some concomitance of elements in his constitution, it is a probable inference that he has the corresponding complexion of skin. For the same disposition of bodily elements, which in the former instance was momentarily present in the case of an access of shame, might be a result of a man's natural temperament, so as to produce the corresponding colouring also as a natural characteristic. All conditions, therefore, of this kind, if caused by certain permanent and lasting affections, are called affective qualities. For pallor and duskiness of complexion are called qualities, inasmuch as we are said to be such and such in virtue of them, not only if they originate in natural constitution, but also if they come about through long disease or sunburn, and are difficult to remove, or indeed remain throughout life. For in the same way we are said to be such and such because of these.

Those conditions, however, which arise from causes which may easily be rendered ineffective or speedily removed, are called, not qualities, but affections: for we are not said to be such in virtue of them. The man who blushes through shame is not said to be a constitutional blusher, nor is the man who becomes pale through fear said to be constitutionally pale. He is said rather to have been affected.

Thus such conditions are called affections, not qualities. In like manner there are affective qualities and affections of the soul. That temper with which a man is born and which has its origin in certain deep-seated affections is called a quality. I mean such conditions as insanity, irascibility, and so on: for people are said to be mad or irascible in virtue of these. Similarly those abnormal psychic states which are not inborn, but arise from the concomitance of certain other elements, and are difficult to remove, or altogether permanent, are called qualities, for in virtue of them men are said to be such and such.

Those, however, which arise from causes easily rendered ineffective are called affections, not qualities. Suppose that a man is irritable when vexed: he is not even spoken of as a bad-tempered man, when in such circumstances he loses his temper somewhat, but rather is said to be affected. Such conditions are therefore termed, not qualities, but affections.

The fourth sort of quality is figure and the shape that belongs to a thing; and besides this, straightness and curvedness and any other qualities of this type; each of these defines a thing as being such and such. Because it is triangular or quadrangular a thing is said to have a specific character, or again because it is straight or curved; in fact a thing's shape in every case gives rise to a qualification of it.

Rarity and density, roughness and smoothness, seem to be terms indicating quality: yet these, it would appear, really belong to a class different from that of quality. For it is rather a certain relative position of the parts composing the thing thus qualified which, it appears, is indicated by each of these terms. A thing is dense, owing to the fact that its parts are closely combined with one another; rare, because there are interstices between the parts; smooth, because its parts lie, so to speak, evenly; rough, because some parts project beyond others.

There may be other sorts of quality, but those that are most properly so called have, we may safely say, been enumerated.

These, then, are qualities, and the things that take their name from them as derivatives, or are in some other way dependent on them, are said to be qualified in some specific way. In most, indeed in almost all cases, the name of that which is qualified is derived from that of the quality. Thus the terms 'whiteness', 'grammar', 'justice', give us the adjectives 'white', 'grammatical', 'just', and so on.

There are some cases, however, in which, as the quality under consideration has no name, it is impossible that those possessed of it should have a name that is derivative. For instance, the name given to the runner or boxer, who is so called in virtue of an inborn capacity, is not derived from that of any quality; for both those capacities have no name assigned to them. In this, the inborn capacity is distinct from the science, with reference to which men are called, e.g. boxers or wrestlers. Such a science is classed as a disposition; it has a name, and is called 'boxing' or 'wrestling' as the case may be, and the name given to those disposed in this way is derived from that of the science. Sometimes, even though a name exists for the quality, that which takes its character from the quality has a name that is not a derivative. For instance, the upright man takes his character from the possession of the quality of integrity, but the name given him is not derived from the word 'integrity'. Yet this does not occur often.

We may therefore state that those things are said to be possessed of some specific quality which have a name derived from that of the aforesaid quality, or which are in some other way dependent on it.

One quality may be the contrary of another; thus justice is the contrary of injustice, whiteness of blackness, and so on. The things, also, which are said to be such and such in virtue of these qualities, may be contrary the one to the other; for that which is unjust is contrary to that which is just, that which is white to that which is black. This, however, is not always the case. Red, yellow, and such colours, though qualities, have no contraries.

If one of two contraries is a quality, the other will also be a quality. This will be evident from particular instances, if we apply the names used to denote the other categories; for instance, granted that justice is the contrary of injustice and justice is a quality, injustice will also be a quality: neither quantity, nor relation, nor place, nor indeed any other category but that of quality, will be applicable properly to injustice. So it is with all other contraries falling under the category of quality.

Qualities admit of variation of degree. Whiteness is predicated of one thing in a greater or less degree than of another. This is also the case with reference to justice. Moreover, one and the same thing may exhibit a quality in a greater degree than it did before: if a thing is white, it may become whiter.

Though this is generally the case, there are exceptions. For if we should say that justice admitted of variation of degree, difficulties might ensue, and this is true with regard to all those qualities which are dispositions. There are some, indeed, who dispute the possibility of variation here. They maintain that justice and health cannot very well admit of variation of degree themselves, but that people vary in the degree in which they possess these qualities, and that this is the case with grammatical learning and all those qualities which are classed as dispositions. However that may be, it is an incontrovertible fact that the things which in virtue of these qualities are said to be what they are vary in the degree in which they possess them; for one man is said to be better versed in grammar, or more healthy or just, than another, and so on.

The qualities expressed by the terms 'triangular' and 'quadrangular' do not appear to admit of variation of degree, nor indeed do any that have to do with figure. For those things to which the definition of the triangle or circle is applicable are all equally triangular or circular. Those, on the other hand, to which the same definition is not applicable, cannot be said to differ from one another in degree; the square is no more a circle than the rectangle, for to neither is the definition of the circle appropriate. In short, if the definition of the term proposed is not applicable to both objects, they cannot be compared. Thus it is not all qualities which admit of variation of degree.

Whereas none of the characteristics I have mentioned are peculiar to quality, the fact that likeness and unlikeness can be predicated with reference to quality only, gives to that category its distinctive feature. One thing is like another only with reference to that in virtue of which it is such and such; thus this forms the peculiar mark of quality.

We must not be disturbed because it may be argued that, though proposing to discuss the category of quality, we have included in it many relative terms. We did say that habits and dispositions were relative. In practically all such cases the genus is relative, the individual not. Thus knowledge, as a genus, is explained by reference to something else, for we mean a knowledge of something. But particular branches of knowledge are not thus explained. The knowledge of grammar is not relative to anything external, nor is the knowledge of music, but these, if relative at all, are relative only in virtue of their genera; thus grammar is said be the knowledge of something, not the grammar of something; similarly music is the knowledge of something, not the music of something.

Thus individual branches of knowledge are not relative. And it is because we possess these individual branches of knowledge that we are said to be such and such. It is these that we actually possess: we are called experts because we possess knowledge in some particular branch. Those particular branches, therefore, of knowledge, in virtue of which we are sometimes said to be such and such, are themselves qualities, and are not relative. Further, if anything should happen to fall within both the category of quality and that of relation, there would be nothing extraordinary in classing it under both these heads.

SECTION-3

Part-9

Action and affection both admit of contraries and also of variation of degree. Heating is the contrary of cooling, being heated of being cooled, being glad of being vexed. Thus they admit of contraries. They also admit of variation of degree: for it is possible to heat in a greater or less degree; also to be heated in a greater or less degree. Thus action and affection also admit of variation of degree. So much, then, is stated with regard to these categories.

We spoke, moreover, of the category of position when we were dealing with that of relation, and stated that such terms derived their names from those of the corresponding attitudes.

As for the rest, time, place, state, since they are easily intelligible, I say no more about them than was said at the beginning, that in the category of state are included such states as 'shod', 'armed', in that of place 'in the Lyceum' and so on, as was explained before.

Part-10

The proposed categories have, then, been adequately dealt with. We must next explain the various senses in which the term 'opposite' is used. Things are said to be opposed in four senses: (i) as correlatives to one another, (ii) as contraries to one another, (iii) as privatives to positives, (iv) as affirmatives to negatives.

Let me sketch my meaning in outline. An instance of the use of the word 'opposite' with reference to correlatives is afforded by the expressions 'double' and 'half'; with reference to contraries by 'bad' and 'good'. Opposites in the sense of 'privatives' and 'positives' are 'blindness' and 'sight'; in the sense of affirmatives and negatives, the propositions 'he sits', 'he does not sit'.

(i) Pairs of opposites which fall under the category of relation are explained by a reference of the one to the other, the reference being indicated by the preposition 'of' or by some other preposition. Thus, double is a relative term, for that which is double is explained as the double of something. Knowledge, again, is the opposite of the thing known, in the same sense; and the thing known also is explained by its relation to its opposite, knowledge. For the thing known is explained as that which is known by something, that is, by knowledge. Such things, then, as are opposite the one to the other in the sense of being correlatives are explained by a reference of the one to the other.

(ii) Pairs of opposites which are contraries are not in any way interdependent, but are contrary the one to the other. The good is not spoken of as the good of the bad, but as the contrary of the bad, nor is white spoken of as the white of the black, but as the contrary of the black. These two types of opposition are therefore distinct. Those contraries which are such that the subjects in which they are naturally present, or of which they are predicated, must necessarily contain either the one or the other of them, have no intermediate, but those in the case of which no such necessity obtains, always have an intermediate. Thus disease and health are naturally present in the body of an animal, and it is necessary that either the one or the other should be present in the body of an animal. Odd and even, again, are predicated of number, and it is necessary that the one or the other should be present in numbers. Now there is no intermediate between the terms of either of these two pairs. On the other hand, in those contraries with regard to which no such necessity obtains, we find an intermediate. Blackness and whiteness are naturally present in the body, but it is not necessary that either the one or the other should be present in the body, inasmuch as it is not true to say that everybody must be white or black. Badness and goodness, again, are predicated of man, and of many other things, but it is not necessary that either the one quality or the other should be present in that of which they are predicated: it is not true to say that everything that may be good or bad must be either good or bad. These pairs of contraries have intermediates: the intermediates between white and black are grey, sallow, and all the other colours that come between; the intermediate between good and bad is that which is neither the one nor the other.

Some intermediate qualities have names, such as grey and sallow and all the other colours that come between white and black; in other cases, however, it is not easy to name the intermediate, but we must define it as that which is not either extreme, as in the case of that which is neither good nor bad, neither just nor unjust.

(iii) 'privatives' and 'positives' have reference to the same subject. Thus, sight and blindness have reference to the eye. It is a universal rule that each of a pair of opposites of this type has reference to that to which the particular 'positive' is natural. We say that that is capable of some particular faculty or possession has suffered privation when the faculty or possession in question is in no way present in that in which, and at the time at which, it should naturally be present. We do not call that toothless which has not teeth, or that blind which has not sight, but rather that which has not teeth or sight at the time when by nature it should. For there are some creatures which from birth are without sight, or without teeth, but these are not called toothless or blind.

To be without some faculty or to possess it is not the same as the corresponding 'privative' or 'positive'. 'Sight' is a 'positive', 'blindness' a 'privative', but 'to possess sight' is not equivalent to 'sight', 'to be blind' is not equivalent to 'blindness'. Blindness is a 'privative', to be blind is to be in a state of privation, but is not a 'privative'. Moreover, if 'blindness' were equivalent to 'being blind', both would be predicated of the same subject; but though a man is said to be blind, he is by no means said to be blindness.

To be in a state of 'possession' is, it appears, the opposite of being in a state of 'privation', just as 'positives' and 'privatives' themselves are opposite. There is the same type of antithesis in both cases; for just as blindness is opposed to sight, so is being blind opposed to having sight.

That which is affirmed or denied is not itself affirmation or denial. By 'affirmation' we mean an affirmative proposition, by 'denial' a negative. Now, those facts which form the matter of the affirmation or denial are not propositions; yet these two are said to be opposed in the same sense as the affirmation and denial, for in this case also the type of antithesis is the same. For as the affirmation is opposed to the denial, as in the two propositions 'he sits', 'he does not sit', so also the fact which constitutes the matter of the proposition in one case is opposed to that in the other, his sitting, that is to say, to his not sitting.

It is evident that 'positives' and 'privatives' are not opposed each to each in the same sense as relatives. The one is not explained by reference to the other; sight is not sight of blindness, nor is any other preposition used to indicate the relation. Similarly blindness is not said to be blindness of sight, but rather, privation of sight. Relatives, moreover, reciprocate; if blindness, therefore, were a relative, there would be a reciprocity of relation between it and that with which it was correlative. But this is not the case. Sight is not called the sight of blindness.

That those terms which fall under the heads of 'positives' and 'privatives' are not opposed each to each as contraries, either, is plain from the following facts: Of a pair of contraries such that they have no intermediate, one or the other must needs be present in the subject in which they naturally subsist, or of which they are predicated; for it is those, as we proved, in the case of which this necessity obtains, that have no intermediate. Moreover, we cited health and disease, odd and even, as instances. But those contraries which have an intermediate are not subject to any such necessity. It is not necessary that every substance, receptive of such qualities, should be either black or white, cold or hot, for something intermediate between these contraries may very well be present in the subject. We proved, moreover, that those contraries have an intermediate in the case of which the said necessity does not obtain. Yet when one of the two contraries is a constitutive property of the subject, as it is a constitutive property of fire to be hot, of snow to be white, it is necessary determinately that one of the two contraries, not one or the other, should be present in the subject; for fire cannot be cold, or snow black. Thus, it is not the case here that one of the two must needs be present in every subject receptive of these qualities, but only in that subject of which the one forms a constitutive property. Moreover, in such cases it is one member of the pair determinately, and not either the one or the other, which must be present.

In the case of 'positives' and 'privatives', on the other hand, neither of the aforesaid statements holds good. For it is not necessary that a subject receptive of the qualities should always have either the one or the other; that which has not yet advanced to the state when sight is natural is not said either to be blind or to see. Thus 'positives' and 'privatives' do not belong to that class of contraries which consists of those which have no intermediate. On the other hand, they do not belong either to that class which consists of contraries which have an intermediate. For under certain conditions it is necessary that either the one or the other should form part of the constitution of every appropriate subject. For when a thing has reached the stage when it is by nature capable of sight, it will be said either to see or to be blind, and that in an indeterminate sense, signifying that the capacity may be either present or absent; for it is not necessary either that it should see or that it should be blind, but that it should be either in the one state or in the other. Yet in the case of those contraries which have an intermediate we found that it was never necessary that either the one or the other should be present in every appropriate subject, but only that in certain subjects one of the pair should be present, and that in a determinate sense. It is, therefore, plain that 'positives' and 'privatives' are not opposed each to each in either of the senses in which contraries are opposed.

Again, in the case of contraries, it is possible that there should be changes from either into the other, while the subject retains its identity, unless indeed one of the contraries is a constitutive property of that subject, as heat is of fire. For it is possible that that that which is healthy should become diseased, that which is white, black, that which is cold, hot, that which is good, bad, that which is bad, good. The bad man, if he is being brought into a better way of life and thought, may make some advance, however slight, and if he should once improve, even ever so little, it is plain that he might change completely, or at any rate make very great progress; for a man becomes more and more easily moved to virtue, however small the improvement was at first. It is, therefore, natural to suppose that he will make yet greater progress than he has made in the past; and as this process goes on, it will change him completely and establish him in the contrary state, provided he is not hindered by lack of time. In the case of 'positives' and 'privatives', however, change in both directions is impossible. There may be a change from possession to privation, but not from privation to possession. The man who has become blind does not regain his sight; the man who has become bald does not regain his hair; the man who has lost his teeth does not grow a new set.

(iv) Statements opposed as affirmation and negation belong manifestly to a class which is distinct, for in this case, and in this case only, it is necessary for the one opposite to be true and the other false.

Neither in the case of contraries, nor in the case of correlatives, nor in the case of 'positives' and 'privatives', is it necessary for one to be true and the other false. Health and disease are contraries: neither of them is true or false. 'Double' and 'half' are opposed to each other as correlatives: neither of them is true or false. The case is the same, of course, with regard to 'positives' and 'privatives' such as 'sight' and 'blindness'. In short, where there is no sort of combination of words, truth and falsity have no place, and all the opposites we have mentioned so far consist of simple words.

At the same time, when the words which enter into opposed statements are contraries, these, more than any other set of opposites, would seem to claim this characteristic. 'Socrates is ill' is the contrary of 'Socrates is well', but not even of such composite expressions is it true to say that one of the pair must always be true and the other false. For if Socrates exists, one will be true and the other false, but if he does not exist, both will be false; for neither 'Socrates is ill' nor 'Socrates is well' is true, if Socrates does not exist at all.

In the case of 'positives' and 'privatives', if the subject does not exist at all, neither proposition is true, but even if the subject exists, it is not always the fact that one is true and the other false. For 'Socrates has sight' is the opposite of 'Socrates is blind' in the sense of the word 'opposite' which applies to possession and privation. Now if Socrates exists, it is not necessary that one should be true and the other false, for when he is not yet able to acquire the power of vision, both are false, as also if Socrates is altogether non-existent.

But in the case of affirmation and negation, whether the subject exists or not, one is always false and the other true. For manifestly, if Socrates exists, one of the two propositions 'Socrates is ill', 'Socrates is not ill', is true, and the other false. This is likewise the case if he does not exist; for if he does not exist, to say that he is ill is false, to say that he is not ill is true. Thus it is in the case of those opposites only, which are opposite in the sense in which the term is used with reference to affirmation and negation, that the rule holds good, that one of the pair must be true and the other false.

Part-11

That the contrary of a good is an evil is shown by induction: the contrary of health is disease, of courage, cowardice, and so on. But the contrary of an evil is sometimes a good, sometimes an evil. For defect, which is an evil, has excess for its contrary, this also being an evil, and the mean, which is a good, is equally the contrary of the one and of the other. It is only in a few cases, however, that we see instances of this: in most, the contrary of an evil is a good.

In the case of contraries, it is not always necessary that if one exists the other should also exist: for if all become healthy there will be health and no disease, and again, if everything turns white, there will be white, but no black. Again, since the fact that Socrates is ill is the contrary of the fact that Socrates is well, and two contrary conditions cannot both obtain in one and the same individual at the same time, both these contraries could not exist at once: for if that Socrates was well was a fact, then that Socrates was ill could not possibly be one.

It is plain that contrary attributes must needs be present in subjects which belong to the same species or genus. Disease and health require as their subject the body of an animal; white and black require a body, without further qualification; justice and injustice require as their subject the human soul.

Moreover, it is necessary that pairs of contraries should in all cases either belong to the same genus or belong to contrary genera or be themselves genera. White and black belong to the same genus, colour; justice and injustice, to contrary genera, virtue and vice; while good and evil do not belong to genera, but are themselves actual genera, with terms under them.

Part-12

There are four senses in which one thing can be said to be 'prior' to another. Primarily and most properly the term has reference to time: in this sense the word is used to indicate that one thing is older or more ancient than another, for the expressions 'older' and 'more ancient' imply greater length of time.

Secondly, one thing is said to be 'prior' to another when the sequence of their being cannot be reversed. In this sense 'one' is 'prior' to 'two'. For if 'two' exists, it follows directly that 'one' must exist, but if 'one' exists, it does not follow necessarily that 'two' exists: thus the sequence subsisting cannot be reversed. It is agreed, then, that when the sequence of two things cannot be reversed, then that one on which the other depends is called 'prior' to that other.

In the third place, the term 'prior' is used with reference to any order, as in the case of science and of oratory. For in sciences which use demonstration there is that which is prior and that which is posterior in order; in geometry, the elements are prior to the propositions; in reading and writing, the letters of the alphabet are prior to the syllables. Similarly, in the case of speeches, the exordium is prior in order to the narrative.

Besides these senses of the word, there is a fourth. That which is better and more honourable is said to have a natural priority. In common parlance men speak of those whom they honour and love as 'coming first' with them. This sense of the word is perhaps the most far-fetched.

Such, then, are the different senses in which the term 'prior' is used.

Yet it would seem that besides those mentioned there is yet another. For in those things, the being of each of which implies that of the other, that which is in any way the cause may reasonably be said to be by nature 'prior' to the effect. It is plain that there are instances of this. The fact of the being of a man carries with it the truth of the proposition that he is, and the implication is reciprocal: for if a man is, the proposition wherein we allege that he is true, and conversely, if the proposition wherein we allege that he is true, then he is. The true proposition, however, is in no way the cause of the being of the man, but the fact of the man's being does seem somehow to be the cause of the truth of the proposition, for the truth or falsity of the proposition depends on the fact of the man's being or not being.

Thus the word 'prior' may be used in five senses.

Part-13

The term 'simultaneous' is primarily and most appropriately applied to those things the genesis of the one of which is simultaneous with that of the other; for in such cases neither is prior or posterior to the other. Such things are said to be simultaneous in point of time. Those things, again, are 'simultaneous' in point of nature, the being of each of which involves that of the other, while at the same time neither is the cause of the other's being. This is the case with regard to the double and the half, for these are reciprocally dependent, since, if there is a double, there is also a half, and if there is a half, there is also a double, while at the same time neither is the cause of the being of the other.

Again, those species which are distinguished one from another and opposed one to another within the same genus are said to be 'simultaneous' in nature. I mean those species which are distinguished each from each by one and the same method of division. Thus the 'winged' species is simultaneous with the 'terrestrial' and the 'water' species. These are distinguished within the same genus, and are opposed each to each, for the genus 'animal' has the 'winged', the 'terrestrial', and the 'water' species, and no one of these is prior or posterior to another; on the contrary, all such things appear to be 'simultaneous' in nature. Each of these also, the terrestrial, the winged, and the water species, can be divided again into subspecies. Those species, then, also will be 'simultaneous' in point of nature, which, belonging to the same genus, are distinguished each from each by one and the same method of differentiation.

But genera are prior to species, for the sequence of their being cannot be reversed. If there is the species 'water-animal', there will be the genus 'animal', but granted the being of the genus 'animal', it does not follow necessarily that there will be the species 'water-animal'.

Those things, therefore, are said to be 'simultaneous' in nature, the being of each of which involves that of the other, while at the same time neither is in any way the cause of the other's being; those species, also, which are distinguished each from each and opposed within the same genus. Those things, moreover, are 'simultaneous' in the unqualified sense of the word which come into being at the same time.

Part-14

There are six sorts of movement: generation, destruction, increase, diminution, alteration, and change of place.

It is evident in all but one case that all these sorts of movement are distinct each from each. Generation is distinct from destruction, increase and change of place from diminution, and so on. But in the case of alteration it may be argued that the process necessarily implies one or other of the other five sorts of motion. This is not true, for we may say that all affections, or nearly all, produce in us an alteration which is distinct from all other sorts of motion, for that which is affected need not suffer either increase or diminution or any of the other sorts of motion. Thus alteration is a distinct sort of motion; for, if it were not, the thing altered would not only be altered, but would forthwith necessarily suffer increase or diminution or some one of the other sorts of motion in addition; which as a matter of fact is not the case. Similarly that which was undergoing the process of increase or was subject to some other sort of motion would, if alteration were not a distinct form of motion, necessarily be subject to alteration also. But there are some things which undergo increase but yet not alteration. The square, for instance, if a gnomon is applied to it, undergoes increase but not alteration, and so it is with all other figures of this sort. Alteration and increase, therefore, are distinct.

Speaking generally, rest is the contrary of motion. But the different forms of motion have their own contraries in other forms; thus destruction is the contrary of generation, diminution of increase, rest in a place, of change of place. As for this last, change in the reverse direction would seem to be most truly its contrary; thus motion upwards is the contrary of motion downwards and vice versa.

In the case of that sort of motion which yet remains, of those that have been enumerated, it is not easy to state what is its contrary. It appears to have no contrary, unless one should define the contrary here also either as 'rest in its quality' or as 'change in the direction of the contrary quality', just as we defined the contrary of change of place either as rest in a place or as change in the reverse direction. For a thing is altered when change of quality takes place; therefore either rest in its quality or change in the direction of the contrary may be called the contrary of this qualitative form of motion. In this way becoming white is the contrary of becoming black; there is alteration in the contrary direction, since a change of a qualitative nature takes place.

Part-15

The term 'to have' is used in various senses. In the first place it is used with reference to habit or disposition or any other quality, for we are said to 'have' a piece of knowledge or a virtue. Then, again, it has reference to quantity, as, for instance, in the case of a man's height; for he is said to 'have' a height of three or four cubits. It is used, moreover, with regard to apparel, a man being said to 'have' a coat or tunic; or in respect of something which we have on a part of ourselves, as a ring on the hand: or in respect of something which is a part of us, as hand or foot. The term refers also to content, as in the case of a vessel and wheat, or of a jar and wine; a jar is said to 'have' wine, and a corn-measure wheat. The expression in such cases has reference to content. Or it refers to that which has been acquired; we are said to 'have' a house or a field. A man is also said to 'have' a wife, and a wife a husband, and this appears to be the most remote meaning of the term, for by the use of it we mean simply that the husband lives with the wife.

Other senses of the word might perhaps be found, but the most ordinary ones have all been enumerated.

THE END

www.ingramcontent.com/pod-product-compliance
Lightning Source LLC
LaVergne TN
LVHW101933220826
846093LV00009B/446